The Usborne
CHRISTMAS TREASURY

First published in 2001 by Usborne Publishing Ltd., Usborne House,
83-85 Saffron Hill, London EC1N 8RT, England. www.usborne.com

The Usborne
CHRISTMAS TREASURY

Edited by Michelle Bates, Jenny Tyler
and Fiona Watt

Designed by Andrea Slane and Lucy Owen

Stories retold by Heather Amery

Illustrated by
Brenda Haw, Stephen Cartwright,
Norman Young and Amanda Barlow

Photography by Howard Allman

Contents

Christmas songs and carols

The Christmas story

Mary lived with her husband, Joseph, very
long ago in the town of Nazareth. Joseph was
a carpenter. Mary was expecting a baby. An
angel had told her she would have a son.

Mary and Joseph had to go to Bethlehem to
register to pay their taxes. They loaded up
their donkey with food and water, warm
clothes and things for the baby.
Then they set out on the long journey
which took many weeks.
The roads were rough and stony.
Joseph had to walk all the way
so that Mary could
ride on the donkey.

When, at last, they reached
Bethlehem, it was late in the evening.
The town was noisy and crowded with people
who had come to pay their taxes. Mary and
Joseph walked through the streets, trying to
find somewhere to stay for the night, but there
were no empty rooms.

Joseph knocked on the door of the last inn.
"All the rooms are taken," said the innkeeper,
"but you can sleep in that stable if you
like. It's dry and clean."

Joseph led Mary to the stable. He
made a bed of soft hay for her on
the floor, covering it with his cloak.
Mary was very tired. She lay down,
thankful that she could rest at last.
Joseph brought her food and
water for her supper.

That night, Mary's baby was born.
She washed him and wrapped him in the
clothes she had brought with her. Joseph
filled a manger with clean hay to make a bed
for the new baby and Mary laid him gently in
it. She called her little son Jesus. The angel
had told her that this was
his name and that he
was the son of God.

Out on the hills near Bethlehem, a band of shepherds lay around their campfire, guarding their flocks of sheep through the night. There were wolves in the hills which prowled around in the dark, trying to snatch a sheep or a lamb.

Suddenly, the night sky was filled with the most brilliant light. The shepherds woke up, staring at the light. "What's that, what's that?" shouted one. Then they saw an angel, and were very frightened.

"Don't be frightened," said the angel. "I have wonderful news for you, and for all people. Tonight the son of God, who is Christ the Lord, was born in a stable in Bethlehem." Then the sky filled with angels, singing the praises of God. As the shepherds watched, the light faded and the sky grew dark again. "We must go to Bethlehem," said one of them, and they hurried down the hills to the town.

The shepherds soon found the stable and, knocking on the door, crept quietly in. They looked at the baby in the manger and knelt down in front of him. They told Mary and Joseph what the angel had said to them.

After some time, the shepherds left the stable and made their way through the streets, telling everyone they met that the son of God had been born that night.

Soon the whole town had heard about the birth of Jesus. Filled with great excitement and singing praises to God, the shepherds walked back to their sheep on the dark hills outside Bethlehem.

Far away to the East of Bethlehem,
three Wise Men saw a new, very bright star
moving across the sky. They knew that it meant
something special had happened. They decided
that a new ruler had been born, and that they
must follow the star to go and find him.

They soon began the long journey, taking presents for the new ruler. They followed the star as it moved across the night sky. They reached the great city of Jerusalem, but no one could tell them about the baby. The star moved on until it stopped over Bethlehem.

The Wise Men soon found Mary and Joseph.
When they saw baby Jesus, they knelt down,
and gave Mary the presents of gold,
frankincense and myrrh they had brought with
them. Then they went quietly home.

A few nights later, Joseph had a dream. In it an angel warned him that Jesus was in great danger. He and Mary and Jesus quickly left Bethlehem on the long journey to Egypt. After many months, they returned to their home in Nazareth where they were safe at last.

The Story of Saint Nicholas

Saint Nicholas lived hundreds of years ago in the city of Myra, which is in Turkey. He was a bishop, and was known to be a very wise, kind old man.

One morning, when he was walking through the streets of the city, he saw three pretty girls sitting in the doorway of a house, looking very miserable. The youngest was crying.

Saint Nicholas stopped and talked to them. "What is the matter?" he asked kindly.

"We are in terrible trouble," said one. "We're sisters, and we were all engaged to be married, but because we have no money for our dowries, our fiancés' families have cancelled the weddings. We have nowhere to go, and will have to beg in the streets." The other two sisters began to cry too.

"Oh dear, oh dear, I wish I could help you," murmured Saint Nicholas, and went on his way, thinking hard.

He had no money but he knew plenty of rich merchants 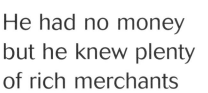 who did. Quietly, he visited them, and told them the sad story of the three sisters. When he went home that afternoon, his pockets were heavy with gold.

In the evening, after dark, he went out and silently dropped three bags of gold through the window of the house where the sisters lived.

In the morning, when they found the gold, they were overjoyed. Now they could get married.

Everyone in the city heard about the three bags of gold, and was delighted. No one knew where such riches came from, but some nodded knowingly to each other. From then on, when anyone had a gift that seemed to come from nowhere, they said it must come from good, kind Saint Nicholas.

Although he lived so long ago, we still remember Saint Nicholas or Saint Niclaus. Now we call him Santa Claus when he brings us presents at Christmas.

Santa Claus

Santa Claus is known by lots of different names around the world. He's called père Noël in France, papai Noel in Brazil, Saint Nicolas in Belgium and in many places, just Father Christmas.

The name Santa Claus comes from the Dutch word for Saint Nicholas, "Sinterklaas". The red and white suit that he wears is similiar to that of the traditional Turkish bishop's robes that Saint Nicholas wore.

It is said that Santa Claus lives near the North Pole and flies through the sky on a sleigh pulled by reindeer. The most famous of his reindeer is Rudolph, whose bright red nose is supposed to help Santa see his way in the dark.

A visit from Saint Nicholas

'Twas the night before Christmas,
when all through the house
Not a creature was stirring, not even a mouse;
The stockings were hung by the chimney with care,
In hopes that Saint Nicholas soon would be there;

The children were nestled
all snug in their beds,
While visions of sugar-plums
danced in their heads;

And mamma in her 'kerchief, and I in my cap,
Had just settled down for a long winter's nap,
When out on the lawn
there arose such a clatter,
I sprang from the bed to see
what was the matter.

Away to the window
I flew like a flash,
Tore open the shutters
and threw up the sash.

The moon on the breast
of the new-fallen snow
Gave the lustre of mid-day
to objects below,
When, what to my wondering
eyes should appear,
But a miniature sleigh,
and eight tiny reindeer,
With a little old driver,
so lively and quick,
I knew in a moment
it must be Saint Nick.

More rapid than eagles
his coursers they came,
And he whistled, and shouted,
and called them by name;

"Now, Dasher! now, Dancer!
now, Prancer and Vixen!

On, Comet! on Cupid!
on, Donder and Blitzen!

To the top of the porch!
to the top of the wall!

Now dash away! dash away! dash away all!"

As dry leaves that before the wild hurricane fly,
When they meet with an obstacle, mount to the sky,
So up to the house-top the coursers they flew,
With the sleigh full of toys, and Saint Nicholas too.
And then, in a twinkling, I heard on the roof
The prancing and pawing
of each little hoof.

As I drew in my hand,
and was turning around,
Down the chimney
Saint Nicholas came with a bound.

He was dressed all in fur, from his head to his foot,
And his clothes were all tarnished
with ashes and soot;
A bundle of toys he had flung on his back,
And he looked like a peddler
just opening his pack.
His eyes – how they twinkled!
his dimples how merry!
His cheeks were like roses,
his nose like a cherry!
His droll little mouth was
drawn up like a bow,
And the beard of his chin
was as white as the snow;
The stump of a pipe
he held tight in his teeth,
And the smoke it encircled
his head like a wreath;

He had a broad face and a little round belly,
That shook, when he laughed like a bowlful of jelly.
He was chubby and plump,
a right jolly old elf,
And I laughed when I saw him,
in spite of myself;
A wink of his eye
and a twist of his head,
Soon gave me to know
I had nothing to dread;

He spoke not a word,
but went straight to his work,
And filled all the stockings; then turned with a jerk,
And laying his finger aside of his nose,
And giving a nod, up the chimney he rose;
He sprang to his sleigh, to his team gave a whistle,
And away they all flew like the down of a thistle.
But I heard him exclaim, ere he drove out of sight,
"MERRY CHRISTMAS TO ALL, AND TO ALL
A GOOD-NIGHT."   Clement Clarke Moore

The story of Cinderella

Once upon a time, there was a young girl named Cinderella. She lived in a big house with her father, who was often away from home, her horrible stepmother and her two mean stepsisters. They hated her because she was pretty and because she was always kind and good-tempered.

The horrible stepmother
and mean stepsisters made
Cinderella do all the work in the house. She
cleaned and cooked from
morning until bedtime. They
made her sit in the
kitchen, gave her only
scraps of food and old
clothes to wear. Her

bedroom was in the cold, creepy attic.
Cinderella was very unhappy, but she had no
one she could talk to about it.

One day, Cinderella and the two stepsisters
received invitations to the Christmas Ball at
the Palace. The stepsisters screamed with
excitement. "We must look our very best for
the Prince," shrieked one. "We'll need very
expensive lovely new dresses and new shoes,
and new bags and gloves," shouted the other.
"Let's start at once."

When the great day came, the two stepsisters spent hours and hours getting dressed and doing their hair. "Don't I look gorgeous?" screamed one. "I know I look perfectly lovely," shrieked the other. At last, when they were ready to leave, Cinderella asked quietly, "Please may I come?" "No, of course you can't. Stay in the kitchen where you belong," shouted both the stepsisters. Off they went, slamming the door behind them.

Cinderella sat in the kitchen and cried.
Suddenly she heard a voice, "I am your fairy
godmother. What's the matter, my dear?" She
looked up and saw somebody standing in front
of her. "I was invited to the Ball, and I did so
want to go," said Cinderella. "Dry your tears.
Do as I say, and you shall go," said her fairy
godmother, smiling.

"Now," she said, "bring me a big pumpkin from the garden, six white mice, the cage with a brown rat in it from the shed, and six green lizards from behind the water tub."
Cinderella couldn't think why her fairy godmother wanted all these things, but she ran as fast as she could to collect them. "Take them outside, please," said her fairy godmother.

The fairy godmother tapped each one in turn with her magic wand.

Cinderella gasped as, in a twinkling, the big pumpkin turned into a grand coach.

Another tap and a twinkle, and the six white mice turned into six white horses.

Then the rat turned into a fine coachman, and the six lizards into six smart footmen.

The fairy godmother tapped Cinderella's old clothes and her shoes with her wand. In another twinkling, they had turned into a lovely dress and shining glass slippers.

"Go to the Ball, my dear," said the fairy godmother, "but remember, you must leave before the clock strikes midnight."

"Oh, thank you," cried Cinderella.

Cinderella drove to the Ball in her
grand coach, and the Prince came
out to meet her. Everyone thought she was a
Princess and even her stepsisters didn't
recognize her. There was a wonderful supper
and music all evening.

The Prince danced every dance with Cinderella. The stepsisters were angry and grew more and more furious with every second that passed.

Cinderella was so happy she forgot all about the time. Suddenly she heard the clock strike midnight. "I must go," she cried, and ran out of the ballroom and down the stairs, losing one of her slippers on the way.

As she ran out of the palace, her dress turned to rags and the coach into a pumpkin. She ran on and was sitting in the kitchen when her stepsisters came home. They told her all about the Ball and the strange Princess who suddenly ran away.

The next morning, the Prince was very sad. He wanted to see the girl he'd danced with again, but he didn't even know her name. All he had was her slipper. "I will search until I find her," he said. "Every girl must try on the slipper. The one whose foot it fits, shall be my bride."

For days, he went from house to house. Many girls tried on the slipper but it was always too small for them. At last he came to Cinderella's house. The stepsisters tried to put it on. They pushed and pulled, heaved and tugged, but the slipper was too small.

Cinderella watched them. "May I try?" she asked. "No, you can't," screamed the stepsisters. "Let her try," said the Prince, smiling. Of course, the slipper was a perfect fit. At that moment, the fairy godmother appeared and Cinderella's rags turned into a lovely dress.

"I've found you at last. Will you marry me?" cried the Prince. "Oh, yes please," said Cinderella, very happily. "Oh no," the stepsisters screamed. Soon the Prince and Cinderella were married. They lived in the Palace and were always happy.

The story of the Nutcracker

"Look, Drosselmeyer's here!" Clara Stahlbaum and her brother, Fritz, looked out of the window. It was Christmas Eve and the street outside their house was covered in snow. All over Germany, families and friends were celebrating and guests had already started to arrive at the Stahlbaum house. Clara and Fritz rushed to the front door to greet their godfather.

Herr Drosselmeyer bent down to give the children a big hug. No one knew exactly what he did. Some people said that he was an inventor, while others thought that he was an explorer. Whatever he was, there was something very magical about him.

"Merry Christmas, Drossy!" Clara and Fritz's mother rushed over to greet their godfather. Then, they all went into the dining room where the other guests were gathered around a Christmas tree. "The most beautiful Christmas tree in the world," Clara thought, with its little white lights and, at the top of the tree, the most beautiful ornament – the Sugar Plum Fairy.

"I've brought some presents for you," Drosselmeyer exclaimed. Hurriedly, Fritz ripped the paper from his package. "Fantastic!" he cried when he saw the golden trumpet inside. Carefully, Clara untied the string around hers to find a wooden soldier.

"It's not just any old soldier, Clara," Drosselmeyer said, "It's a nutcracker." And, popping a hazelnut into the soldier's mouth, he tapped it on the head. Instantly the shell of the nut cracked in two. Clara was delighted.

"Let me see," said Fritz. Reluctantly, Clara handed over her present. Fritz forced a huge nut into the soldier's jaws and smacked its head down with a loud bang. "Now look what you've done," Clara cried as a crack stretched across the soldier's face. "It'll be all right," her mother said. "We'll mend him in the morning." Clara walked over to her cradle of dolls and laid her nutcracker inside.

*

Clara couldn't get to sleep that night. She kept thinking about the nutcracker. Would her mother really be able to mend him? Eventually she decided to look again to see how bad the crack in his face really was. Quickly, she crept out of bed, tiptoed downstairs and pushed back the door to the drawing room. She walked over to her cradle of dolls... just as the clock struck twelve.

Suddenly there was a noise from behind and Clara turned to see the most horrible sight – a huge mouse, getting bigger and bigger by the the minute. On its head was a crown, and in its hand there was a sword. As it rose on its hind legs, the room suddenly filled with scurrying mice.

Clara jumped up onto the sofa. Before she even had a chance to think what to do next, the nutcracker sprang into life and stood in front of her, as tall as a man. He was joined by a whole army of soldiers. Clara stared at the soldier in astonishment, noticing that he didn't have a crack across his face any more.

"Attack!" the Mouse King cried, pointing his sword in the air. The most terrible battle then raged. Soldiers and mice whipped and lashed with their swords.

Clara hardly dared breathe as she watched the Mouse King advancing on her soldier. The horrid mouse knocked the sword out of the soldier's hands and pushed him against a wall. Quick as a flash, Clara pulled off her slipper and threw it, as hard as she could, at the back of the Mouse King's head... THWACK! The force of the blow knocked the Mouse King to the floor and the other mice fled.

All the soldiers cheered, and as Clara hugged the soldier with relief, he was transformed into a handsome prince. "You've saved my life," the prince whispered. "In return for your bravery, can I take you to my Kingdom?" Clara gasped, as a sea of waves filled the room. A magical ship appeared and, in a trance, Clara stepped into it. Soon they were sailing through an enchanted forest full of dancing snowflakes.

When Clara and the prince reached the Kingdom of Sweets, festivities were well underway. Crowds lined the streets, celebrating the victory over the mice. Clara stepped down from the ship and looked around her. She could hardly believe what lay before her – it really was a land made of sweets. There were houses made of licorice and street lights made from lollipops. Shimmering groups of dancers appeared before Clara and performed the most wonderful dances from around the world. But, she let out a gasp as the final dancer appeared. It was the beautiful Sugar Plum Fairy from the top of her own Christmas tree. Clara watched, wide-eyed, as the fairy pirouetted through the air.

All too soon the dance was at an end. "Clara," the prince said.

"There isn't much time if you want to be home in time for Christmas morning, but before you go, I want to thank you for saving my life by making a wish come true for you." Clara took a deep breath. "I wish I could dance like the Sugar Plum Fairy." Clara glanced at her feet and found she was wearing a beautiful pair of ballet shoes. She stepped forward, took the prince's hand and began to dance. As the music came to an end, Clara looked behind her and saw the sea whipping up waves. "It's time to go home," the prince whispered, leading her back to the ship. The sky filled with snow and Clara closed her eyes.

*

When Clara opened her eyes, she was no longer on the ship, but back home on the sofa. The nutcracker, a prince no more, was lying beside her. The house was quiet and, for a moment, Clara thought that she had been dreaming. But then she looked down at the nutcracker and saw that his face was no longer cracked.

The Little Fir Tree

The Little Fir Tree grew in the middle of a clearing in the forest. It was a very small fir tree, and it didn't like being small.

It would sigh as it looked at all the other trees around it. They grew so quickly while it grew so very, very slowly. The Little Fir Tree was so unhappy, it didn't notice how the wind blew through its branches, how the sun warmed its needles, and how the rain fell gently on it.

Every winter, when the snow lay thick on the ground, men would come and cut down the tall fir trees. They loaded them onto carts and dragged them away. The Little Fir Tree wondered where they were being taken, and wanted to go with them. It asked the stork, "What happens to those great trees?"

"Some are made into the masts of ships. I've seen them sailing across the seas," answered the stork. The Little Fir Tree didn't know what ships or seas were, but it hoped that, one day, it would be a mast. That sounded wonderful.

Year after year, the Little Fir Tree grew in the clearing – slowly getting taller and taller. One winter's day, men came with carts and horses.

"This one will do nicely," said a man, digging around the Little Fir Tree's roots. "What's happening?" the Little Fir Tree wondered.

The men lifted up the Little Fir Tree, pushed its roots into a big tub, and packed soil all around it. Then they hoisted the tub onto a cart with lots of other trees, and drove away. "Where am I going?" wondered the Little Fir Tree.

The men drove the cart through the forest to a town. The Little Fir Tree stared at all the houses, the people, and the Christmas decorations in the streets. The cart stopped outside a big house, and a girl and a boy came running out, followed by a man. Everyone crowded around the cart to look at it.

The Little Fir Tree shook its branches. It felt so tall and proud, standing in its tub. "Look at that tree, it's perfect," cried the girl. "It's just the right size." "Please may we have it, Dad?" asked the boy. "Yes, we'll take that one," said the man.

He gave the cart driver some money, and the Little Fir Tree was carried into the house, and put in the corner of a big room.

Later that day, the children's mother came into the room with their granny and auntie. They put little lights all over the Little Fir Tree, then they hung shining glass balls, tinsel and pretty angels all over its branches. Auntie climbed up a stepladder, and put a silver star at the very top of the tree. Then they all piled presents underneath the Little Fir Tree and stood back and gazed at it.

"It looks lovely. Just wait until the children see it," said Mother. "Now we're all ready for Christmas," said granny. They switched on the lights, and went out, leaving the Little Fir Tree alone again.

Suddenly, the door opened and lots of children rushed into the room, chattering and laughing with excitement.

"Look at the tree, look at the tree," they shouted, dancing around it. The room was full of noise and laughter, and the Little Fir Tree stood with all its lights glowing. It felt so proud and happy. It knew that it looked beautiful.

At last, the children went out of the room. The Little Fir Tree could hear them in the dining room with the grown-ups, eating and drinking, talking and laughing.

In the evening, an old man put a chair by the Little Fir Tree, and sat down. All the children came in and sat on the floor around him. When it was quiet the old man began to tell the children stories. The Little Fir Tree listened; he had never heard such wonderful stories.

Then it was time for bed. Just before one little girl scampered out of the door, she turned and looked at the tree again. "It's the most wonderful Christmas tree ever," she said, and then she quietly closed the door.

The Little Fir Tree stood alone in the corner. Its lights had been switched off, but all the decorations and the silver star on the topmost branch gleamed in the light of the street lamp outside the window. The Little Fir Tree sighed. "I'm a Christmas tree. That's much better than being a mast. I wish all the trees in the forest could see me now," it thought. "This is the happiest day of my life."

Christmas traditions

Every year, people all over the world celebrate Jesus' birthday on December 25th. They celebrate in lots of ways and many different traditions have sprung up.

Hanging stockings

The practice of hanging stockings on Christmas Eve first began with Saint Nicholas, when he left gifts of gold coins in the stockings of three poor girls. In Holland, Dutch children put out shoes rather than stockings, to receive gifts.

Christmas cards

People first sent Christmas cards over a hundred and fifty years ago. These usually showed pictures of Mary, Joseph and baby Jesus.

Christmas presents

Some people give presents to their family and friends on Jesus' birthday – December 25th. In some countries they give them on January 6th which is called Epiphany and is the day that the Three Wise Men are said to have visited Jesus.

Christmas trees

The tradition of putting up a Christmas tree began in Germany in the early Middle Ages. The first Christmas tree in Britain was probably brought over from Germany by Prince Albert, for his wife, Queen Victoria, and their children. The star at the top of a Christmas tree represents the Star of Bethlehem that guided the Three Wise Men to Jesus.

Christmas pudding

It is traditional to have Christmas pudding in England. The first Christmas puddings were made of dried fruit, flour and spices. Each member of the family took part in the making of the pudding, and made a wish. Christmas desserts in North America include fruitcake, mince pie and pumpkin pie.

Boxing Day

The name Boxing Day is thought to come from an old practice of opening collection boxes in churches on December 26th. The money from the boxes was given to poor people.

Pop-up Christmas card

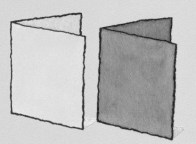

1. Cut two rectangles of paper the same size. Fold them in half like this, to make two cards.

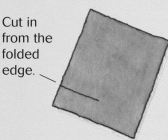

Cut in from the folded edge.

2. Cut a slit halfway across one of the cards, like this. Keep the card folded as you cut.

This part will be the tree.

3. Lift the paper above the cut and fold it over onto the front of the card. Crease the fold well.

4. Turn the card over and crease the tree the other way. Then, open the card and lay it flat.

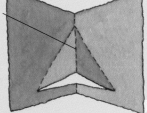

Crease this fold.

5. Push a finger through the tree from the back so that it stands up. Pinch along the middle fold.

6. Carefully close the card, so that the tree lies flat inside it. Crease all the folds really well.

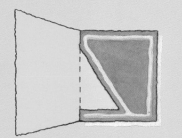

7. Glue around the edge of the tree card. Press it inside the other card, matching the middles.

8. Use felt-tip pens, stickers and paper to decorate inside the card. Decorate the front too.

If you don't use green paper for the card, glue green paper onto the tree. Add shapes cut from paper on the background.

For a card with three trees, make three cuts at step 2.

For a trunk, fold a piece of paper in half. Glue it below the tree, matching the folds.

Starry wrapping paper

1. Draw a star on a piece of thin cardboard and cut it out. Use a pencil to draw around it lots more times on the cardboard.

2. Cut out the stars. Put a small blob of poster tack in the middle of each one. Press half of them onto a large piece of paper.

3. Pour some pale paint onto an old plate. Dip a sponge into the paint and dab all over the paper. Leave it to dry.

Sponge over holly leaf shapes instead of stars.

Try sponging gold acrylic paint over a dark shade of paint.

4. Clean the plate and sponge. When the paint is dry put the remaining stars into the spaces on the paper.

5. Put some darker paint onto the plate and sponge it on. Make sure that all of the paper is covered with paint.

6. When the paint is dry, carefully peel off all the stars. As you do it, you will reveal star shapes all over the paper.

For a gift tag, sponge over a star on a piece of thin cardboard.

Sparkling decorations

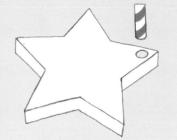

1. Press a big cookie cutter firmly into a slice of bread, then press the shape out of the cutter.

2. Press the end of straw into the shape to make a hole. Don't make the hole too close to the edge.

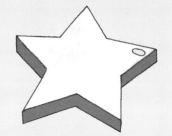

3. Make more bread shapes. Leave them on a baking rack overnight. They will harden.

4. Mix a little paint with some household glue (PVA). Paint it along the edges of the shapes.

5. Paint the top of the shapes. When the paint is dry, turn them over and paint the other side.

6. Glue lots of glitter onto each side of the shapes. You could glue on tiny beads and sequins, too.

7. Push a long piece of thick thread through the hole. Make a loop in the end of the thread.

8. Push the ends of the thread through the loop to make a knot. Pull the knot tight.

Make lots of
decorations using
different shapes of
cookie cutters.

These bread
shapes are for
decorations only.
Don't eat them.

Hanging decorations

To make about 20 decorations, you will need:
50g (4 tablespoons) light soft brown sugar
50g (4 tablespoons) butter, softened
a small egg
130g (½cup) plain flour
1 teaspoon ground mixed spice
solid boiled sweets or hard candy
a large star-shaped cookie cutter
a fat drinking straw
a small round cutter, slightly bigger than the sweets
a large baking sheet lined with baking parchment

Heat the oven to 180°C, 350°F, gas mark 4

Use sweets or candy which are about the same size as the round cutter you use.

1. Turn on your oven. Put the butter and sugar into a bowl. Use a wooden spoon to mix them together really well.

2. Break the egg into a separate bowl. Beat it with a fork until the white and the yolk are mixed together well.

3. Mix half of the beaten egg into the mixture, a little at a time. You don't need the other half of the beaten egg.

4. Sift the flour and the mixed spice through a sieve. Mix everything together with a wooden spoon.

5. Squeeze the mixture really well with your hands to make a firm dough. Then, make it into a large ball.

6. Sprinkle a clean work surface with flour. Put the dough onto it, then roll out the dough until it is 5mm (¼in) thick.

These are best as decorations. You can eat them, but the middles are very hard.

7. Using a large cookie cutter, press out lots of star shapes. Use a spatula to put them on the baking sheet.

8. Make a small hole in each star by pressing the straw through the dough near the top of one of the points.

9. Use a small, round cookie cutter or a clean bottle top to cut out a hole in the middle of each star.

Thread a thin ribbon through the hole.

10. Bake the stars on the middle shelf of the oven for five minutes. Then, carefully take the baking sheet out of the oven.

11. Drop a sweet or candy into the hole in the middle of each star shape. Be very careful as the baking sheet will be hot.

12. Bake the stars for five more minutes. Leave them on the baking sheet until they have cooled completely.

Snowman Christmas card

Fold back.   Fold back.

1. Fold a piece of white paper in half, short sides together. Fold each edge back to meet the first fold, making a zigzag.

2. Keeping the paper folded, draw an outline of a snowman. Make the arms and toes touch the sides of the paper.

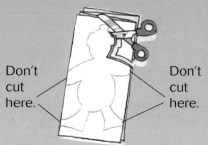

Don't cut here.   Don't cut here.

3. With the paper still folded, cut around the snowman shape. Don't cut along the ends of the arms and toes.

4. Unfold the paper carefully and lay it flat. Use felt-tip pens to draw faces, hats and scarves on the snowmen.

5. For the backing card, cut a piece of paper the same size as the white paper you started with. Fold it in half.

6. Unfold the backing card and lay it flat. Put glue on the back of the first and last snowmen in the chain.

Middle folds

7. Lay the chain across the backing card, making sure that the middle folds line up. Press down the two end snowmen.

8. Carefully close the card, pulling the middle fold toward you. When you open it the middle snowmen will stand out.

9. For snowy grass, fold a thin strip of paper into a zigzag, as in step 1. Cut a grassy outline. Glue it inside the card as before.

Try different shapes. Remember not to cut along the folded edges.

Peppermint creams

- a Christmas gift idea

For about 25 peppermint creams, you will need:
250g (1 cup) icing sugar*, sifted
half the white of a small egg (mixed from
egg white substitute, as directed on the package)
2 teaspoons lemon juice
half a teaspoon of peppermint essence
red food dye
a baking sheet covered in plastic foodwrap
small cutters
rolling pin

1. Sift the icing sugar through a sieve into a deep bowl. Make a hole in the middle of the sugar with a spoon.

2. In a small bowl, mix the egg white, the lemon juice and the peppermint. Pour the mixture into the hole in the sugar.

You can use any shape of small cutter.

3. Use a blunt knife to stir the mixture. Then, squeeze the mixture between your fingers until it is really smooth.

*in US = powdered sugar

4. Cut the mixture into two pieces. Put each piece into a bowl. Add a few drops of red food dye to one bowl.

5. Stir in the dye, then squeeze it with your hands until the dye is mixed in. Add some more of the sugar if the mixture gets sticky.

6. Sprinkle a little of the sugar onto a clean, smooth work surface. Sprinkle some sugar onto a rolling pin as well.

7. Roll each mixture until it is as thick as your little finger. Use the cutter to cut out lots of shapes. Cut them close together.

8. Use a blunt knife to lift the shapes onto a baking sheet. Leave them for at least an hour until they become hard.

For a present, put tissue paper into a giftbox and put the peppermint creams on top.

Coconut mice

- another Christmas gift idea

To make about 15 mice, you will need:
250g (1⅓ cups) icing sugar*
200g (8oz) can of condensed milk
175g (fl cup) desiccated coconut
red food dye
licorice 'bootlaces'
silver cake decorating balls
chocolate buttons
plastic foodwrap

1. Put the icing sugar and the condensed milk into a bowl and mix them with a spoon. Then, add the coconut and mix it in.

2. Share the mixture between two bowls. Mix in a few drops of food dye to each bowl to make two shades of pink.

3. Dip a tablespoon into some water and let the water drip off it. Then, lift out a big spoonful of one of the mixtures.

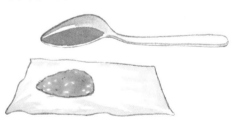

4. Pat the spoonful smooth on top. Turn the spoon over and put the coconut shape onto a piece of plastic foodwrap.

5. Gently pinch the thinner end of the shape to make a nose. Press in chocolate buttons for ears and silver balls for eyes.

6. For a tail, press in a piece of licorice under the body. Make lots more mice. Leave them on a plate to harden.

*in US = powdered sugar

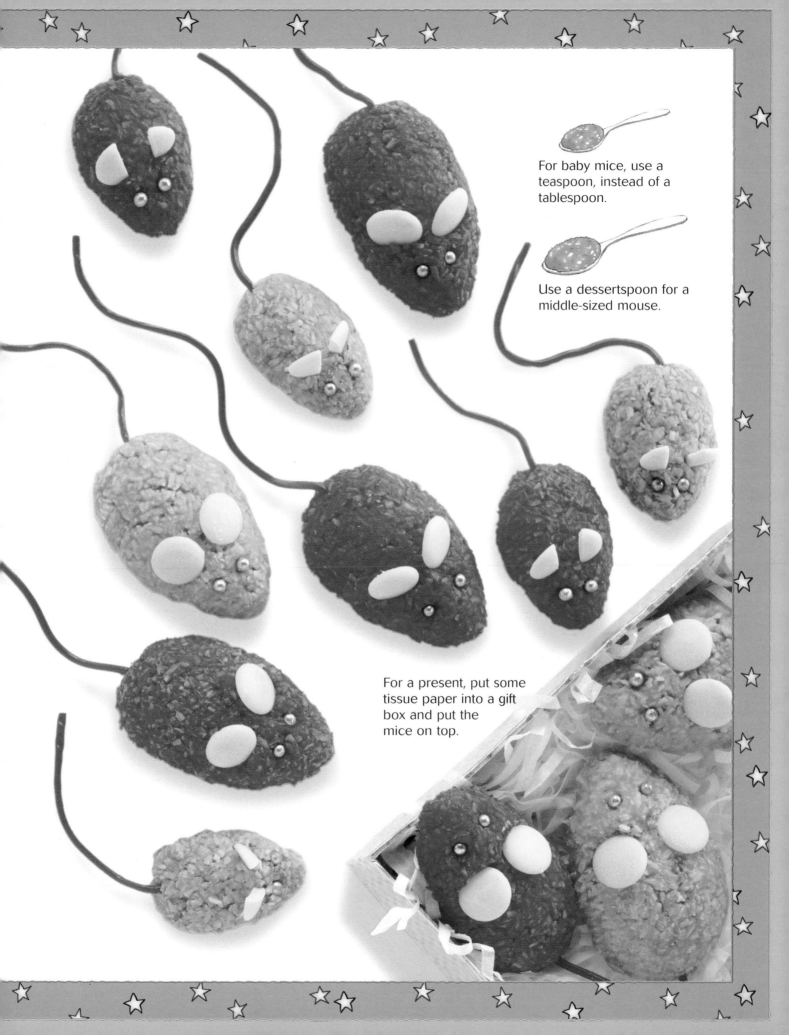

For baby mice, use a teaspoon, instead of a tablespoon.

Use a dessertspoon for a middle-sized mouse.

For a present, put some tissue paper into a gift box and put the mice on top.

The twelve days of Christmas

On the first day of Christ-mas, my true love sent to me A

part-ridge in a pear tree. On the sec-ond day of Christ-mas, my

true love sent to me Two tur-tle doves and a part-ridge in a pear

tree. On the third day of Christ-mas, my true love sent to me

Three French hens, two turtle doves and a partridge in a pear tree. On the fourth day of Christmas my true love sent to me Four calling birds, three French hens, two turtle doves, and a partridge in a pear tree. On the fifth day of Christmas my

On the first day of Christmas,
my true love sent to me
A partridge in a pear tree.

On the second day of Christmas, my true love sent to me
Two turtle doves and a partridge in a pear tree.

On the third day of Christmas, my true love sent to me
Three French hens, two turtle doves
and a partridge in a pear tree.

On the fourth day of Christmas, my true love sent to me
Four calling birds, three French hens, two turtle doves
and a partridge in a pear tree.

true love sent to me Five gold_ rings, four cal - ling birds, three French hens

two tur - tle doves and a part - ridge_ in a pear tree. On the

sixth
seventh
eighth
ninth day of Christ - mas my true love sent to me
tenth
eleventh
twelfth

On the fifth day of Christmas, my true love sent to me
Five gold rings, four calling birds...

On the sixth day of Christmas, my true love sent to me
Six geese a laying, five gold rings...

On the seventh day of Christmas, my true love sent to me
Seven swans a swimming, six geese a laying...

On the eighth day of Christmas, my true love sent to me
Eight maids a milking, seven swans a swimming...

Six   geese   a   lay - ing,   five   gold_____ rings,
Seven   swans   a   swim - ming,
Eight   maids   a   milk - ing,
Nine   lad - ies   danc - ing,
Ten   lords   a   leap - ing,
Eleven   pip - ers   pip - ing,
Twelve   drum - mers   drum - ming,

four_____ call - ing birds,   three French hens   two_____ tur - tle doves   and   a

part - ridge_____ in   a   pear   tree.   On   the   tree

On the ninth day of Christmas, my true love sent to me
Nine ladies dancing, eight maids a milking...

On the tenth day of Christmas, my true love sent to me
Ten lords a leaping, nine ladies dancing...

On the eleventh day of Christmas, my true love sent to me
Eleven pipers piping, ten lords a leaping...

On the twelfth day of Christmas, my true love sent to me
Twelve drummers drumming, eleven pipers piping...

O little town of Bethlehem

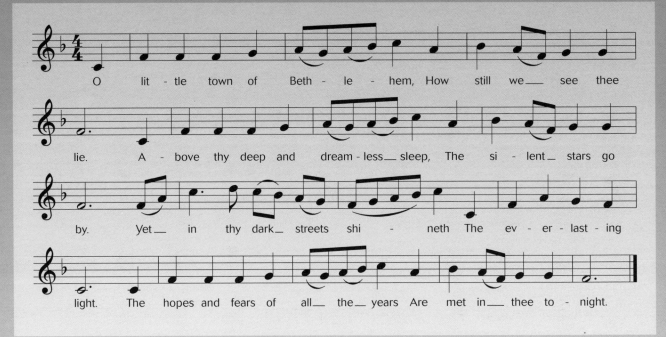

O morning stars, together
Proclaim thy holy birth.
And praises sing to God the King
And peace to men on Earth.
For Christ is born of Mary
And, gathered all above
While mortals sleep, the angels keep
Their watch of wondering love.

How silently, how silently,
The wondrous gift is given!
So God imparts to human hearts
The blessings of his heaven.
No ear may hear his coming,
But in this world of sin,
Where meek souls will receive him, still
The dear Christ enters in.

O holy child of Bethlehem,
Descend to us we pray,
Cast out our sin, and enter in,
Be born in us today.
We hear the Christmas angels
The great glad tidings tell:
O come to us, abide with us,
Our Lord Emmanuel.

Jingle bells

A day or two ago
I thought I'd take a ride
And soon Miss Fannie Bright
Was seated by my side;
The horse was lean and lank,
Misfortune seem'd his lot,
He got into a drifted bank,
And then we got upsot!

Oh, jingle bells, jingle bells,
Jingle all the way.
Oh what fun it is to ride
In a one-horse open sleigh.
Oh, jingle bells, jingle bells,
Jingle all the way.
Oh what fun it is to ride
In a one-horse open sleigh.

I saw three ships

I saw three ships come sail - ing by, on Christ - mas Day, on

Christ - mas Day, I saw three ships come sail - ing by, On

Christ - mas day in the mor - ning. And mor - ning.

And what was in those ships all three?
On Christmas Day, on Christmas Day,
And what was in those ships all three?
On Christmas Day in the morning.

Our Saviour Christ and his lady.
On Christmas Day, on Christmas Day,
Our Saviour Christ and his lady.
On Christmas Day in the morning.

Silent night

Si - lent night, ho - ly night, All is calm,

all is bright; Round yon vir - gin, moth - er and child,

Ho - ly in - fant so ten - der and mild, Sleep in hea - ven - ly

peace, Sleep in hea - ven - ly peace.

Silent night, holy night,
Son of God, love's pure light;
Radiance beams from thy holy face,
With the dawn of redeeming grace,
Jesus, Lord at thy birth,
Jesus, Lord at thy birth.

Silent night, holy night,
Shepherds wake at the sight;
Glory streams from heaven afar,
Heavenly hosts sing Alleluia.
Christ the saviour is born!
Christ the saviour is born!

While shepherds watched their flocks

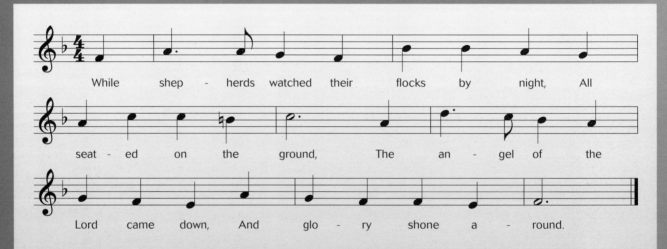

While shep - herds watched their flocks by night, All seat - ed on the ground, The an - gel of the Lord came down, And glo - ry shone a - round.

"Fear not," said he; for mighty dread
Had seized their troubled mind;
"Glad tidings of great joy I bring
To you and all mankind."

"To you in David's town this day
Is born of David's line
A Saviour, who is Christ the Lord;
And this shall be the sign:"

"The heavenly Babe you there shall find
To human view displayed
All meanly wrapped in swathing bands,
And in a manger laid."

Thus spake the seraph; and forthwith
Appeared a shining throng
Of angels praising God, who thus
Addressed their joyful song:

"All glory be to God on high,
And to the Earth be peace;
Goodwill henceforth from heaven to men
Begin and never cease."

Away in a manger

The cattle are lowing, the baby awakes,
But little Lord Jesus, no crying he makes.
I love thee Lord Jesus; look down from the sky,
And stay by my side until morning is nigh.

Be near me Lord Jesus; I ask thee to stay
Close by me forever and love me, I pray;
Bless all the dear children in thy tender care,
And fit us for heaven to live with thee there.

We three Kings of Orient are

We three Kings of O - ri - ent are,

Bear - ing gifts we tra - vel so far, Field and

foun - tain, moor and moun - tain, Fol - low - ing

yon - der star. O_____ star of won - der,

star of night, Star with roy - al beau - ty

bright, West - ward lead - ing, still pro - ceed - ding

Guide us to thy per - fect light.

Born a king on Bethlehem's plain,
Gold I bring, to crown him again,
King forever, ceasing never
Over us all to reign.

O star of wonder, star of night...

Frankincense to offer have I,
Incense owns a Deity nigh;
Prayer and praising, all men raising
Worshipping God most high.

O star of wonder, star of night...

Myrrh is mine, its bitter perfume
Breathes a life of gathering gloom;
Sorrowing, sighing, bleeding, dying,
Sealed in a stone-cold tomb.

O star of wonder, star of night...

Glorious now behold him arise,
King and God and sacrifice,
Alleluia, Alleluia;
Earth to the heavens replies.

O star of wonder, star of night...

We wish you a Merry Christmas

We wish you a Mer - ry Christ - mas, We wish you a Mer - ry

Christ - mas, We wish you a Mer - ry Christ - mas, And a Hap - py New

Year. Good tid - ings we bring To you and your kin; We

wish you a Mer - ry Christ - mas And a Hap - py New Year.

We all want some figgy pudding,
We all want some figgy pudding,
We all want some figgy pudding,
So bring some right here!

Good tidings we bring
To you and your kin;
We wish you a Merry Christmas
And a Happy New Year.

We won't go until we get some,
We won't go until we get some,
We won't go until we get some,
So bring some right here!

Good tidings we bring
To you and your kin;
We wish you a Merry Christmas
And a Happy New Year.

The origins of Christmas songs

Silent night

The words for this well-known carol were written in 1816, but the tune was composed two years later by a church organist. Some people think that the organist composed the carol to be played on a guitar because the church organ had broken and could not be repaired in time for Christmas Eve.

Jingle bells

When this popular Christmas song was written in 1857 it was called "The one-horse open sleigh", not "Jingle bells".

While shepherds watched

The original version of "While shepherds watched their flocks by night" is thought to be about 300 years old. Its tune is based on one written by the famous composer, Handel. The tune sung today dates from around 1850.

O little town of Bethlehem

This is an American Christmas carol, written by a bishop who had visited the Holy Land. It was first sung in 1868.

The twelve days of Christmas

This song probably dates back to 1500s. The twelve days begin on Christmas Day and continue until 6th January. It was quite common for wealthy people to give gifts to their family on each of the twelve days.